INSTRUCTIONAL RESOURCES
CENTER
Highline Public Schools
15675 Ambaum Blvd. S.W.
Seattle, WA   98166

P9-EKH-568

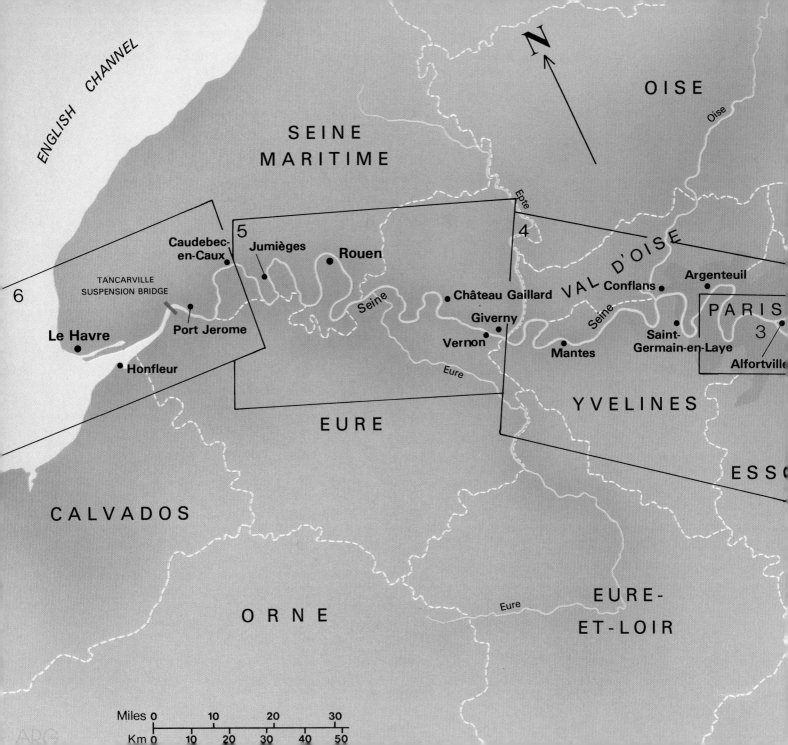

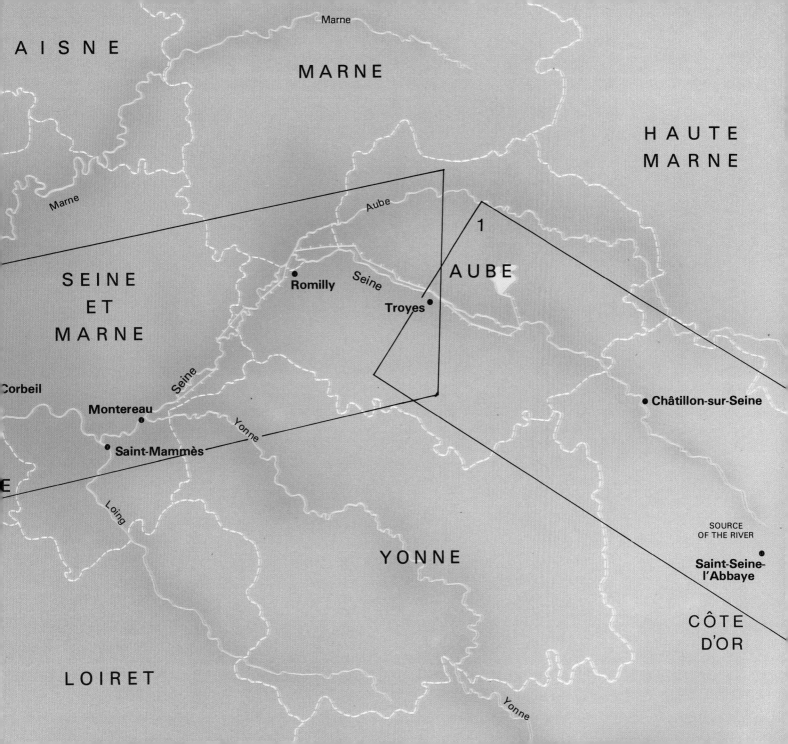

AISNE

MARNE

Marne

HAUTE
MARNE

Marne

SEINE
ET
MARNE

Aube

1

AUBE

Seine

Romilly

Troyes

Corbeil

Seine

Montereau

Yonne

Saint-Mammès

Châtillon-sur-Seine

Loing

YONNE

SOURCE
OF THE RIVER

Saint-Seine-
l'Abbaye

CÔTE
D'OR

LOIRET

Yonne

The Seine

Source of inspiration to artists and writers through the
years, the Seine has not only witnessed much of French
life and culture, but has also enabled Paris to become a
prosperous centre of trade. Many people only know the
stretch of the Seine which flows through Paris, but this
book describes how the little stream bubbles
forth high on the wooded slopes of the Côte-d'Or
in Burgundy, gradually gaining strength as it
gathers the waters of tributary rivers, flowing on
through Paris, and the industrial centres of
Rouen and Le Havre, to meet its final resting
place in the English Channel.

The author takes the reader on a fascinating
journey down France's most famous and
well-loved river, describing the sights en route,
and explaining the importance of the river to the
economy of France.

C. A. R. Hills is an experienced freelance writer
who has degrees in both history and geography.
He has travelled extensively in western Europe
and has also written *The Danube* and *The Rhine* in
this series.

River traffic on the Seine — a pleasure boat steams past barges moored along the river.

Rivers of the World

The Seine

C. A. R. Hills

Wayland/Silver Burdett

Rivers of the World

Amazon

Colorado

Congo

Danube

Euphrates

Ganges

Mekong

Mississippi

Nile

Rhine

Rio Grande

Seine

St Lawrence

Thames

Volga

Yellow River

© Copyright 1981 Wayland Publishers Limited
First published in 1981 by
Wayland Publishers Limited
49 Lansdowne Place, Hove
East Sussex BN3 1HF, England
ISBN 0 85340 807 6

Published in the United States by
Silver Burdett Company
Morristown, New Jersey
1981 printing
ISBN 0 382 06519 0

Phototypeset by Trident Graphics Limited, Reigate, Surrey
Printed in Italy by G. Canale & C.S.p.A., Turin

Contents

Introduction: the smiling river of France

The Seine – the great river of France is classed as one of the world's most important rivers, although it is only a short river by world standards. Witness to so much of French life and culture, it was the Seine which caused the great city of Paris to be built where it now stands. To many Frenchmen, and indeed to many foreigners, Paris sums up everything they feel about France. And it is the Seine, flowing in a great bend through the heart of the city, that is the centre of Parisian life.

Many people know only the relatively small stretch of the Seine which flows through Paris. But the Seine, together with its tributary rivers, such as the Yonne, Aube, Marne and Oise, drains the greater part of the whole area of northern France. Rising in the upland region of Burgundy in the centre of France, the source of the Seine lies close to the area where French rivers divide – streams flowing south to the warm waters of the Mediterranean separate from those flowing north towards the English Channel and the Atlantic.

On its journey to the Channel the Seine flows through fruitful land where low-lying ground, fertile soils and an equable climate have given rise to rich agriculture. Along the banks of the river towns and cities such as Troyes, Mantes, Rouen and Le Havre have prospered through the ages. This low-lying country is shaped like a saucer with different sorts of rocks forming the

Above *The Seine provides many quiet places where people can fish and bathe.*

Right *A barge chugs past the beautiful cathedral of Notre Dame.*

Above *Seurat has captured the lazy atmosphere of the sun-drenched river in this picture of the bathers at Asnières.*

rim – gentle, rounded hills of chalk and limestone alternating with soggy, clay lowlands. Through this landscape the Seine has cut an easy path in a long series of loops. The river meanders its gentle but purposeful way north and then west, passing signs of life both ancient and modern – castles and mansions, fields and woods, orchards and gardens, landing stages and docks, car factories and power stations – all physical reminders of the life and culture that France has developed over many centuries.

Most rivers seem to have developed a character of their own: a quality which somehow seems to spring from the character of the country through which they flow. The Seine is a calm, smoothly-flowing river that rarely seems to menace or threaten the surrounding landscape. Rising at only 471 metres (1545 feet), it does not have far to fall in its journey to the sea, so there are few spectacular rapids or waterfalls. Nor does the Seine receive any waters from ice-covered highlands giving rise to spring floods when the ice melts. Instead its waters come from springs on hillsides, so dangerous floods, obstacles in its course or shifting channels are quite rare. What disturbances there are have been overcome by barrages, reservoirs and weirs. The river expends much of its energy cutting the many loops by which it progresses to the sea. In places it is so placid that there hardly seems to be any current. People standing on the banks of the Seine in Paris are often surprised to see that the river appears to be flowing upstream! The Seine is ideal for river traffic, being navigable along nearly all its course. The only barrier is the relative shallowness of the water in the upper reaches, which prevents large boats penetrating upstream. But from Paris to the sea through the great ports of Rouen and Le Havre, river traffic is very heavy: barges pulled by tugs are as common a sight as great ocean-going ships.

In quieter stretches of the river people wash their clothes, swim and sunbathe, sail lazily in boats, or sit on the banks and paint the river's many moods, as so many famous artists have done. The smooth, glassy waters calmly reflect the changing shades of the overhanging skies; the lines of poplars stand straight along the banks and the willow trees bend gracefully over the waters. The Seine is indeed a smiling river – the smiling river of France.

In the following chapters we shall sail along the river, stopping here and there to admire the view, and to consider the many interesting sights that meet our eyes as we pass along.

Below *One of the many artists painting scenes along the Seine*

From the source to Troyes

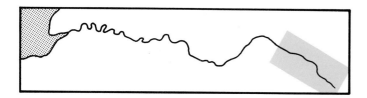

The Seine rises in a remote part of Burgundy on the slopes of a hill called Mont Tasselot in the Côte-d'Or (which means the 'Golden Hillside'). The source is fed by a number of tiny springs forming small pools in a lonely valley on the hillside. Only one winding road leads to the wooded spot where, among tangles of wild flowers and the song of larks, the various springs join together to form the source of the river. The quicksilver stream flowing down the valley is so narrow that a child could jump across it, and in times of drought it may dry up completely, only coming to life again further down the valley.

The source of the Seine is an interesting and mysterious spot, associated with the worship of an ancient goddess. In Roman times, and probably before that, the river's flow was thought to be caused by the river nymph, Sequana. Two thousand years ago the Romans built a great temple in the lonely wood to honour the goddess. A little further down the valley was a long pool where a number of sources of the Seine joined.

Below *This statue of the goddess Sequana marks the source of the Seine amid the wooded glades of Mont Tasselot.*

Above *The Douix pours forth its crystal-clear waters from beneath a sheer limestone cliff above the town of Châtillon-sur-Seine.*

This was used for bathing, because the waters were thought to be holy and to cure all kinds of diseases. Ruins of the Roman temple can still be seen today, together with a more modern monument to the goddess. In 1867 the authorities of the city of Paris erected a statue of Sequana in a grotto above the main spring which feeds the Seine. Beside the statue is a plaque

Above *The picturesque town of Châtillon-sur-Seine has many charming old buildings nestling along the banks of the river.*

explaining that the statue was to honour 'the river to which Paris owes her ancient prosperity'. From under the smiling figure of Sequana the stream bubbles forth, gathering other brooks as it gradually gains strength.

The tiny river flows among thorns and thistles and small meadows. Gradually we begin to see signs of human life, as the river passes several outdoor laundries where women come to wash their clothes in the pure water, allowing their young children to paddle or bathe. After about two kilometres (one mile) we come to the little village of Saint-Seine-l'Abbaye, where half-timbered houses nestle around an ancient abbey. The river then passes through woods of oak, ash and sycamore, where the water is harnessed to work many little water mills. Fishermen stand patiently by the stream waiting to catch some of the many trout which live in these parts.

The first town we come to is Châtillon-sur-Seine. Near here the Seine receives the waters from its first important tributary, the Douix, which pours out in a rush from under a lime-stone cliff. Châtillon suffered damage from Italian bombers during the Second World War, and many of the buildings are of modern gleaming stone. However, many narrow little streets of the old town still survive. To the north of the town is a grassy hill, Mont Lassois, where in January 1953 an archaeological find of immense interest was made. This was the burial mound of a princess who had died 2500 years ago in the sixth century B.C. She had been buried with an ornamental carriage and surrounded by treasures: a gold diadem, bronzes, jewellery, cups, and the greatest treasure of all, the vase of Vix, made of precious bronze and standing 1.64 metres (5½ feet) high. This beautiful vase had in fact been made in faraway Greece. During the Iron Age this part of the Seine lay on some of the most important trade routes along which tin from Britain and many luxury goods from Greece were imported. This prosperous trade must have been one of the reasons why the princess's people could afford to bury such rich treasures with her.

Soon we leave the province of Burgundy and enter that of Champagne – a French province world-famous for its wines, although these are mostly grown in the area to the north of the Seine. Vineyards are in fact a rare sight on the banks of the Seine. The landscape is now changing from the upland country of Burgundy to a wider valley with meadows and bare chalk hillsides set a little way back from the river. The Seine is, however, still a small river as it approaches the town of Troyes. Even the smallest barges cannot penetrate the river this far, although they can travel as far as Troyes by making use of a lateral canal which has been cut beside the Seine.

Troyes is the first important town on the Seine. It began life as a Roman fort, and in the early medieval period, seven or eight hundred years ago, Troyes was one of the most important towns in France. In those days the king of

Above *In the upper reaches of the Seine the local women do their washing in the clean, pure river water.*

France ruled over the whole of France, but in practice many of the local nobles were so powerful that the king's authority was diminished. The Count of Champagne was one of these powerful rulers whose capital was Troyes. The town was famous for the fairs that were held there, when goods from the whole of Europe were bought and

Left *Troyes still has many medieval, half-timbered houses.*

Above *Troyes, the ancient capital of Champagne, was once a city of fairs, jousting tournaments and feasts.*

sold, and for the great jousting tournaments where medieval knights met to prove their strength. But since then the pace of development has somehow passed Troyes by, and it has become a very typical French provincial town – a little sleepy, but beautiful and full of corners of interest. In the old town there are many medieval houses, some with turrets, others with overhanging roofs which almost meet each other above the narrow streets. Unfortunately, a number of these buildings have been allowed to fall into a state of decay, or have been pulled down. But the centre of the town is still very charming, and the atmosphere is enriched by the hundreds of brightly-coloured bicycles that are driven with great speed along the narrow streets.

On the outskirts of Paris

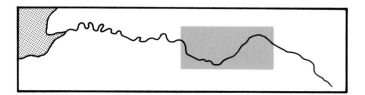

Once we are clear of the rather dreary suburbs of Troyes, we begin travelling through flat, open country. Long rows of tall, straight poplar trees line the banks of the river – a common sight in France. These are usually planted as a timber crop, although they do sometimes grow naturally. At Romilly, a rather dull town mostly noted for its large number of flour mills, the Seine is joined by the River Aube (which at this point is the larger of the two rivers), and turns from flowing northwest to west. The Seine is now 145 km (90 miles) from its source, and is becoming a more powerful stream, carrying small barges and lined with dusty towpaths. We are now in the Île de France, the central province of France, and begin to sense that Paris is near. Just outside Montereau is the town of Surville – one of the new towns built to take overspill population from Paris, where thousands of people now live. The town, which is built on a high plateau, commands a panoramic view of the Seine, and the architecture of the buildings is impressive. But French new towns compare poorly with those built elsewhere in Europe in terms of amenities – if the citizens of Surville want a meal out or to go to the cinema they usually have to go to a nearby town.

Below *This painting by Monet captures the mood of the Seine with long rows of trees fringing the gently-flowing river.*

Above *The Seine is an important commercial link between the port of Le Havre and the city of Paris.*

Signs of modern economic development increase as we travel downriver through a landscape that is partly rural and partly industrial. We see pylons, railways and factory chimneys, as well as an electricity generating station, which is the largest power station in France, supplying much electricity to the European grid. Saint-Mammès is a port and refuelling point for barges, with long lines of quays and permanently oil-stained waters. The next town on our route is Corbeil – a highly industrialized town with the most important grain mills in France as well as a paper mill, a huge printing works and many other large factories. Corbeil is also one of the strongholds of the French Communist Party. This increasingly modern landscape is still interspersed with large farms and endless rows of poplars. Near the great palace of Fontainebleau – used hundreds of years ago by French kings as a hunting lodge – the palace gardens and thick forest stretch towards the river. The forest, which has been carefully conserved includes an

Left *The château of Fontainebleau, one of the largest royal residences in France, was originally used as a royal hunting lodge.*

Above *As the Seine approaches Paris the landscape becomes increasingly urbanized.*

amazing variety of trees: oaks, ashes, beeches, sycamores, chestnuts, and poplars.

As we approach Paris the farms become smaller and more widely spread, and the factory chimneys thicken. At Alfortville, the Seine is joined by its greatest tributary: the majestic Marne. Fortified by these waters the Seine enters Paris and prepares to take a great bend through 13 km (8 miles) of perhaps the most famous river frontage in the world.

The Seine in Paris

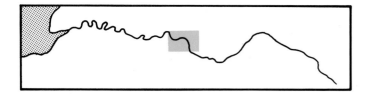

Paris is one of the most important cities in the world – an international place of pilgrimage and second home to many millions of people who are not French. It is also one of the world's largest cities with more than eight million people (about one in five Frenchmen) living in Paris or its suburbs. It is the centre of almost every aspect of French life: government, commerce, industry, culture, entertainment, as well as being a great port. Its many beautiful buildings and famous landmarks are familiar even to those who have never seen them.

Situated in the centre of the fertile Île de France near the meeting of routes to all parts of Europe, Paris is built on an ideal site for a great city. As the Seine approaches Paris it divides round two islands, the Île de la Cité and to the north the Île Saint-Louis. The first settlement grew up on the larger of the two islands – the Île de la Cité – which is shaped like a boat. The first settlers were a tribe of Gauls, called the Parisii, living many centuries before Christ. However, it was the Romans who founded the original city when they conquered France two thousand years ago. The Romans called their city *Lutetia*. It was not until the fourth century that the town took

Below *An aerial view of Paris showing how the Seine divides into two arms round the Île de la Cité.*

A wintry view of the Seine taken near the Eiffel Tower.

Above *An eighteenth-century view of Paris showing the Pont de la Tournelle in the background.*

on the name of its original inhabitants and became known as Paris. As the power of the French kings increased, Paris grew to become the most important city of France. For more than a thousand years now French history and life have been tied to this great city. Over the centuries the boundary of the city has grown far from the river, but the area along the Seine remains the centre of Paris where crowds gather and the most famous sights are to be seen. You might say that Paris *is* the Seine.

Before we enter the heart of Paris, the river flows through industrial suburbs, and then passes the Gare de Lyon and the Gare d'Austerlitz – the two famous railway stations standing like sentinels on either side of the river.

The famous waterfront views of Paris show the wide pavement along the river bank, lined with plane trees, where an endless stream of gaily dressed crowds leaf through rows of old books in traditional green boxes. Artists sit and sketch the river's changing moods. At the lower level, beside the water's edge, which can be reached by steps or by boat in places, there is often a cobbled way with trees and fishermen. Beneath the arches of the bridges Parisian beggars (called *clochards*) make their homes, or loving couples find shelter from the occasional shower. Many of the bridges spanning the broadly-flowing river, such as the Pont Alexandre III, are beautifully-decorated with sculptured cupids, scrolls, flower garlands, shells, birds, trumpets and lions. At night the shimmering water reflects the thousand lights of the city of Paris.

But how far is this romantic view of Paris true? Although the waterfront has become heavily commercialized, it is still a place of enjoyment – a beautiful water-park where people can stroll, talk, sunbathe, boat and paint. In the 1960s this peaceful atmosphere was almost destroyed by the building of the new Paris expressway on the Right Bank, bringing a great swathe of petrol-laden traffic through the peace of the scene. But after great public protest, the building of another expressway on the Left Bank was halted, so it is still possible to walk and dream there. On the whole then the romantic picture is surprisingly close to reality.

Above *Tourists leaf through the books and prints on sale along the embankment with the grim Conciergerie in the background.*

Below *The Pont Alexandre III is the most flamboyant of all the bridges across the Seine.*

As we travel down the river, we pass many famous buildings, sights and monuments. The Île de la Cité is the centre of France, and all distances in France are measured from a point on the island. The focal point of the island is the cathedral of Notre Dame. This great building, which was built from 1163 to 1250, is world-famous for its twin towers and the nave with rose-windows beneath. In front of the cathedral is the great square of the Parvis, very large and grand but oddly desolate. Also on the island is the beautiful Sainte Chapelle – once the private chapel of the kings of France – and the sombre Palais de Justice. Towering grimly above the many other old buildings is the fortress of the Conciergerie, which was built in the early fourteenth century. During the French Revolution, when the King was deposed and a Republic set up, many nobles were held in its grim dungeons before being executed. Marie Antoinette, the Queen of France, spent her last hours there before she was sent to the guillotine in 1793. Both the Île de la Cité and the Île Saint-Louis have many beautiful old houses, most of which are now government offices. The oldest bridge across the Seine linking the Île de la Cité

Left *An aerial view of the Île de la Cité crowned by the cathedral of Notre Dame.*

Right *The tree-lined embankments along the Seine are a favourite place for people to pass the time of day.*

Above *An artist's impression of one of the Seine's most graceful bridges, the Pont Royal.*

Right *The night illuminations along the Seine bathe the Conciergerie in warm light, belying its grim past.*

with both the Right and Left Bank is the Pont Neuf (which means 'New Bridge' although it was in fact constructed in 1578!). For two hundred years after it was built, it functioned as a permanent fair, with stalls, singers, acrobats and strolling players.

The Seine divides Paris into two main parts: the Right Bank and Left Bank. Most of the shopping streets and public buildings are on the Right Bank, while the Sorbonne (the University of Paris) and the Latin Quarter, frequented by students and young people, are on the Left Bank. As we travel downstream we pass the Hôtel de Ville (the town hall), and the Louvre, which

extends for over a kilometre along the river bank. The Louvre, which is the largest palace in the world, was built gradually over many centuries from 1202 to 1868. It was originally built as a fortress in the days when Paris lived in fear of attack, but in fact few French rulers ever lived there. Its echoing corridors create a unique effect of austere grandeur, and it houses one of the most famous art galleries in the world. West of the Louvre fronting the river are the famous gardens of the Tuileries (one of the main strolling grounds for Parisians), and the Place de la Concorde, where the guillotine was set up during the Revolution. Later we pass the Trocadero, which houses many of the famous museums of Paris, and the gleaming new radio station built in ultra-modern style. The magnificent Bois de Boulogne marks the boundary of the historic city of Paris.

On the Left Bank the famous sights are a little less thick on the ground, although not far from the river are the narrow streets of the student quarter, the Quartier Latin, and well-preserved Paris quays. Opposite the Trocadero is the Eiffel Tower – perhaps the most famous landmark in Paris. Built on four great swinging arches, it stands 300 metres (984 feet) above the ground, dominating the city from the southwest corner. From the top you can see the city of Paris laid

Left *Colourful barges moored along the Seine remind us that the Seine is one of France's great waterways.*

Above *A quiet day's fishing in the Bois de Boulogne.*

Below *A barge laden with sand makes its way slowly and purposefully up the Seine.*

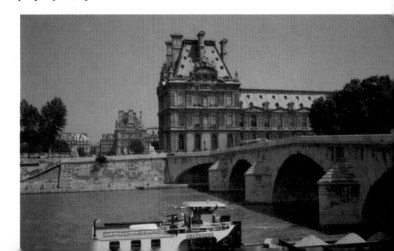

Above *Bookstalls have lined the banks of the Seine for hundreds of years.*

out in all its splendour – across the Right Bank to the hills of Montmartre, topped by the gleaming white church of the Sacré Coeur, and across the Left Bank to the lower hills of Montparnasse.

As we travel on downstream the urban landscape continues, but we have left the historic waterfront behind, and the landscape becomes more everyday, though not less interesting. In the next chapter we shall travel through the suburbs of Paris and the rest of the Île de France.

The gleaming white church of Sacré-Coeur crowns the heights of Montmartre on the Right Bank.

In the Île de France

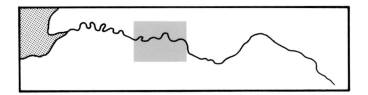

As the Seine leaves Paris it progresses towards the Channel in a series of deep loops round hills. The landscape is becoming predominantly suburban. On our left is the industrial area of Grenelle, full of factories, builders' yards and railway lines, as well as the Citroën and Renault car works. Opposite Grenelle is the highly prosperous suburb of the Seizième, where some of the richest and most exclusive Parisians live: large villas and blocks of luxury flats straggle up the hillside near the Bois de Boulogne. Nearby is the island of La Grande Jatte, which is the subject of a very famous *pointilliste* painting by the great painter, Seurat. This type of picture is made up of thousands of small dots. Seurat's vision of Parisians strolling or sunbathing in a park by the river with chimneys in the distance has become world-famous as a portrayal of how people living cooped up in cities spend their leisure time.

By now the landscape has become industrial and really very ugly. Beside the river are small, often derelict, factories and warehouses, while the banks are laden with rubbish tips and mounds of refuse, which pollute the river and make it smell. In the middle of this wasteland is the suburb of Argenteuil – one of the most often

Below *Barges loading sand and rubble, builders' yards, and skyscrapers line the banks of the Seine in the industrial suburbs of Grenelle.*

Above *Seurat's famous painting* Sunday Afternoon on the Island of La Grande Jatte, *now held by the Art Institute of Chicago.*

painted towns in the world. You may wonder why this town should have been singled out. In the 1870s Paris had not spread this far and the Seine still flowed through rural landscape. During this period a group of painters – Monet, Manet, Renoir, Sisley and Degas (whom we now call the Impressionists) – moved to Argenteuil to paint. Their paintings showed the changing effects of light seen in the reflection of the river. They were mostly poor men – Sisley is said to

Above *The beautiful church of Saint-Denis, where kings and queens of France are buried.*

have been so poor that he could not afford to buy shoes and had to wear sandals all year. When they were not sketching, they spent long hours discussing their new ideas in art. Argenteuil is now a dreary industrial suburb, but the scene they saw – the white square, steeple, bridge and river – can never be erased.

On the very outskirts of suburban Paris is the town of Sèvres, where many of the inhabitants work in the factories producing world-famous Sèvres china. Saint-Denis is another industrial suburb, notable for its beautiful medieval church. At Bougival the landscape becomes more lush. After another bend in the river we come to the forest of Saint-Germain. Here the beautiful hilltop château of Saint-Germain-en-Laye looks out over the river from behind a great terrace of lime trees. This palace has seen much history. Mary Queen of Scots, who was beheaded while a prisoner of Elizabeth I spent

The château of Saint-Germain-en-Laye, standing on a hill above the Seine, was used as a refuge against the Parisian mobs during the French Revolution.

Above *Conflans is a busy barge depot.*

Below *A gaily-decorated barge moored alongside the bargees' church where a wedding is taking place.*

her childhood here. Her great-grandson, James II of England, also lived here until his death after he was deposed in 1688.

At Conflans the Seine is joined by another great tributary, the Oise. Conflans is a loading and refuelling station for barges travelling up and down the Seine. The life of the whole town seems to be dominated by river traffic. The quays are lined with barges, which are often used as houseboats by retired bargees. There is even a church on one of the barges. The Seine carries a great deal of river traffic, most of which is found in the area between Paris and the sea. The amount of river traffic doubled during the 1960s reaching 40,000,000 tonnes in 1975. The barges may be up to 30 metres (100 feet) long and are often pulled in rows by tugs. Barges are the most common form of river traffic near Paris (which is an important port for coal and machinery), but nearer the estuary great ocean-going ships become increasingly common. River traffic on the Seine is an important trade link with the rest of the world, particularly with other members of the European Economic Community. Tributaries of the Seine, such as the Oise, link France with Belgium, while the Marne links France with Germany. There are also canals linking the Seine with other French rivers, such as the Loire and the Rhône. These canals were

Right *The canal Saint-Martin was built to relieve river traffic on the Seine.*

Between Paris and Rouen the Seine flows through wooded farmland. Here the river approaches the industrial town of Mantes.

heavily used when they were first built in the seventeenth century, but are less used now.

Many large rivers have to be extensively excavated by man to allow navigation, but the Seine flows so gently for most of its length that it presents few natural obstructions. The main problem is the frequent loops, but these have been overcome by many cuttings. The thirty-nine barrages, together with locks, help to maintain an adequate depth of water for ships to pass, while a number of reservoirs regulate the flow. In most towns the river flows between dykes and embankments, as a precaution against floods, although these do not occur very often.

We are now passing through rich countryside. Riverside meadows provide grazing land for cattle, and the flourishing market gardens produce food for the city of Paris. Many French people have second homes in this pleasant landscape, and the glittering water is much used for fishing, boating and sailing, while Parisians often come here on excursions during the warm summers. There are many riverside restaurants, often picturesquely set amid chestnut, lime and poplar

Below *A barge moored near a riverside restaurant on the River Oise, tributary of the Seine, at Conflans.*

trees, where the wonders of French provincial cooking can be sampled. But industry and traffic are never far away. As we approach the town of Mantes, traffic builds up, oil and scum float on the surface of the river, and quarries and cement factories churn their effluent into the river. Although fishermen still try to catch any fish that have not died of pollution, there are no washerwomen because the water is too dirty.

The village of Giverny lies at the junction of the River Epte and the Seine. Giverny has become famous, because Monet lived there for forty-three years after his fellow Impressionist painters had left Argenteuil to go their separate ways. At the back of his house was a water-garden spanned by a Japanese bridge which he painted many times. He also painted forty-eight different compositions of the water lilies that grew there. Monet painted eighteen pictures of the Seine trying to catch the light in every mood that the river passed through.

The junction of the Epte and the Seine marks the end of another section of our journey. We have now left the Île de France and are about to enter the rich and beautiful province of Normandy.

Left *The chimneys of an oil refinery near Mantes silhouetted against the sunlit sky.*

Above right *The Water-lily Pond painted in soft greens, blues and yellows by Monet.*

Right *The confluence of the Epte and the Seine near the village of Giverny where Monet spent much of his life.*

The Seine in Normandy

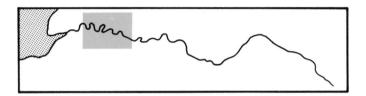

As we enter Normandy the landscape changes subtly. The river has left behind its limestone bed and now flows through chalk country. The landscape has a gentle, rolling aspect with bare patches of chalk often showing through the grass-topped hills. Beneath the chalk are many caves, and even an underground church in one place. Set amid the downland pastures are many villages and towns with flint walls and thatched roofs, apple orchards, and castles and abbeys. This is a rich countryside, which bears the mark of man's influence over the centuries, particularly that of the Normans.

Over a thousand years ago Viking pirates (also known as Northmen and Normans) raided the coast of Europe, robbing and murdering as they went. In 911 their leader, Rollo, signed a treaty with the King of France in which he was given the area of Normandy in return for a promise to settle down. In 1066 one of their dukes, William the Conqueror, became King of England after the Battle of Hastings. The Normans proved themselves efficient farmers, and made Normandy into one of the richest provinces, building villages and towns which have remained to this day. Although Normandy has been part of France for many centuries now, you still see tall, fair-haired people there, who are obviously remote descendants of the Vikings.

First we pass the lovely old town of Vernon.

Below *The remains of the twelfth-century bridge at the lovely village of Vernon.*

The attractive buildings of Les Andelys nestle beneath the white chalk cliffs.

Above *Many of the old, half-timbered houses in the village of Vernon have been carefully restored.*

Hills covered with oak trees and apple orchards fall steeply down to the river which is studded with small, wooded islands. As the Seine turns right round the next bend a dramatic sight meets our eyes – Château Gaillard set high on the top of the highest of a group of gleaming white cliffs.

Château Gaillard means 'Swaggering Castle', which was what it was originally intended to be. It was built by Richard the Lionheart in the 1190s when England and France both claimed that part of France. At that time Richard I held it and intended to build a castle that no one could ever capture. It was the greatest fort in Europe with a keep within a fort within a moat within a keep within outer walls within a moat, all of which was set high on a chalk hill. When the King of France tried to capture the fort from Richard, he sent the following message: 'If the castle's walls were made of iron, yet I would be able to take them!' The English king is said to have replied: 'Tell the French king that, if they were made of butter, yet I would hold them against him and his.' Although the French king failed to capture the castle on that occasion, it did not prove impregnable in later years. In 1204 during the reign of King John of England the castle was captured by the French. For the next two hundred years it swung back and forth between England and France until it was finally captured by the French in 1449. During that time many prisoners were held there and many terrible things happened within its walls. King Louis X of France shut his wife up in the castle,

The ruins of Château Gaillard perched high on the highest of a group of cliffs overlooking the Seine.

Boats moored on the Seine with the church of Petit Andelys in the background.

because she had displeased him. She was kept in a lightless dungeon, where she was murdered when she refused to give her husband a divorce. She is said to have been strangled with her own hair. Later in its history the castle was occupied by bandits who used to capture travellers on the Seine and extort money from them by torturing them. At the end of the sixteenth century King Henry IV decided it was dangerous to have such a powerful fortress in the country, so he had it pulled down. So now it stands, a magnificent ruin, no longer steeped in blood, but with grass and wild flowers growing in its ruined courts, and the Seine and the little town of Les Andelys nestling at its foot. As far as the eye can see the wide woods and fields of Normandy stretch in peace and calm where once its owners used to terrorize.

Near the meeting of the River Andelle and the Seine, stands a steep, grassy hill called *La côte des deux amants* (the hill of the two lovers). There is an interesting legend told about this hill. Long ago a cruel knight, called Rulph, is said to have lived there. He had a daughter called Calixte, who was famous round about because she was so beautiful and fat. She fell in love with a young squire called Raoul, but he was poor and her father would not let her marry him. Then one day Calixte was attacked in a wood by a wild boar, and was saved from certain death by Raoul. As a reward Rulph said the squire could have anything he wished, and Raoul asked to marry Calixte. Rulph was furious, but he

Above The Côte des deux amants *near Rouen – scene of medieval fantasy.*

remembered his promise, and said that he could marry her, if he could carry her to the top of the nearby hill without stopping or dropping her. The squire manfully shouldered the plump burden of Calixte and began to puff up the hill. No one thought he could make it to the top of the hill without dropping her, but he did, only to drop dead of a heart attack as he reached the top. In despair Calixte threw herself off the top of the hill into the Seine.

Above *A nineteenth-century view of Rouen.*

Left *An aerial view of Rouen showing the cathedral.*

Right *Despite the bombing Rouen suffered during the Second World War, many old streets remain such as the* Rue du Gros Horloge.

We leave this scene of medieval fantasy to come to Rouen – a modern town with ancient roots. Rouen was originally a Roman camp, which the Normans chose as their capital. It is one of the busiest and most important ports and cities in France. The city owes its importance as a port to its position on the Seine halfway

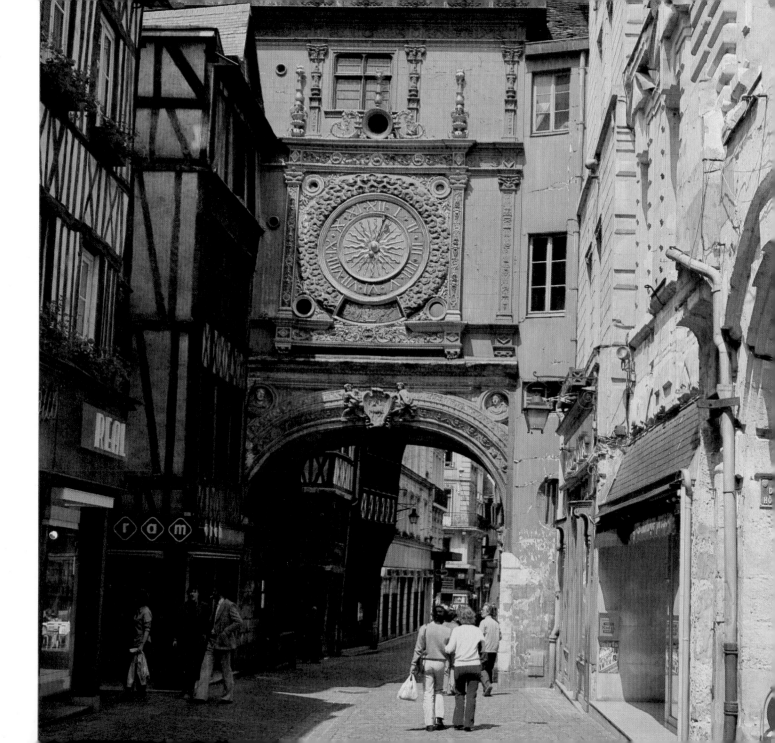

Left *Sunset over the industrial scenery of the port of Rouen.*

Above *Covered barges at Rouen waiting to be unloaded.*

between Paris and the sea. Only 130 km (80 miles) from the sea, Rouen is near the tidal limit, enabling sea-going vessels to reach the city. The quays and wharves of Rouen are always lined with big ships loading and unloading their goods. Tankers take on oil, while wine, timber and cattle are loaded on to ships ready to be transported all over the world. Hundreds of cranes are to be

Above *The modern church of Sainte Jeanne d'Arc — memorial to France's most famous martyr.*

seen by the river and everywhere factory chimneys mingle with church steeples. For Rouen is also a historic city with many fine buildings. It was here that Joan of Arc was convicted of witchcraft and burned at the stake in 1431, after she had led armies into battle against the English. Only a small part of the old town of Rouen remains for the city suffered terrible damage during the Second World War. In 1940 German invaders burned down most of the old quarter, and then in 1944 all the bridges were burned down as the Allies fought to regain control of the city from the Germans. Since then a great modern city has risen from the flames, but the ancient cathedral with its tall spire, the highest in France, still reminds Rouen of its proud past.

As we travel towards the sea, we leave behind the calm of the upper and middle reaches. The river is now tidal and rushes and swirls on its way. Treacherous sandbanks caused by the force of the river current and the rush of the incoming tide makes navigating in small boats tricky. Great ocean-going ships nose their way purposefully through the rural peace of Normandy. This stretch of the river is often known as the *Route des Abbayes* (Route of the Abbeys), because of the many abbeys and churches that were built by the Normans. One of the most famous of these is Jumièges, an early building which predates the Norman period. It became famous as a great centre of learning and culture. However, at the time of the French Revolution the monks were driven out by revolutionaries and it was sold to a Rouen timber merchant, who used it as a warehouse. Naturally it fell into ruins and both the roof and steeple are now missing. It remains a beautiful ruin with its graceful columns standing forlornly among the beech and yew trees.

Right *The beautiful ruin of the Abbey of Jumièges, which was once a great centre of learning.*

Ocean-going ships become increasingly common on the stretch of the Seine between Rouen and Le Havre.

Above *A view across the Seine valley from the* Côte des deux amants *stretching across flat marshland towards the estuary.*

Caudebec-en-Caux is a small town, which used to be very famous for the tidal bore. Four times a year, three days running, twice a day, the wave used to come – a great tower of water travelling at 15 km (9 miles) an hour, attracting sightseers from miles around. Now the channel of the estuary has altered and the bore does not come any longer. But a much smaller bore can sometimes still be seen further up the estuary. The river can be very treacherous in these parts, as it swirls angrily round sandbanks, and most boats need a pilot who knows the waters. At Ville-quier river pilots hand over to estuary pilots. This is officially the place where the Seine estuary begins and the river widens out to meet its final destination in the English Channel.

The Seine estuary and Le Havre

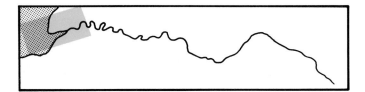

As the Seine reaches its estuary it broadens out amid tidal flats. The polluted river is crowded with ships, and the mudflats are often covered with rubbish as well as old wrecks that have been washed up on the shore. Chimneys and other installations stand out somewhat forlornly in the lonely country. Just before the river widens out the massive oil refineries of Port Jerome with their great white towers, gleaming chimneys and shooting flames shine above the trim hedges and apple trees of the Norman landscape.

Most of the estuary is flat marshland, but there are still a few chalk cliffs. Near one of the last high cliffs is the Tancarville suspension bridge. This great bridge with its beautiful graceful arches stands 48 metres (156 feet) above high tide level and is 1400 metres (4593 feet) long, which makes it one of the longest bridges in Europe. The only bridge across the estuary, it was opened in 1959, and has cut short journey times for people and cargo crossing the estuary. Beyond the bridge desolate marshes stretch into the distance. There are no familiar marshland birds, such as geese, swans or plovers, because the estuary is so polluted by oil and chemicals that wildlife cannot flourish here. Nearby are car

Right *The Tancarville suspension bridge spans the Seine estuary.*

Below *Gleaming oil refineries line the banks of the Seine at Port Jerome.*

Left *Honfleur used to be the Seine's main seaport, but nowadays the only boats moored along the quayside are small fishing boats.*

Above *Cows graze on the marshy flatlands of the Seine estuary.*

factories and the plant where natural gas from the Sahara desert arrives by ship. In the distance loom the towers and wharves of the great port of Le Havre.

As the estuary widens to meet the English Channel, the two river banks form a V-shape. On the left of the estuary is the older port of Honfleur. In the Middle Ages this was a great sea-going port, but from about the seventeenth century it declined in importance due to shifting sandbanks and the silting up of the harbour. But it has remained a charming little town with many sleepy old streets. In the bars along the harbour fishermen and yachtsmen exchange idle gossip to while away the hours.

In complete contrast on the opposite bank stands Le Havre. The greatest and busiest port in France – a title which it took from Marseilles

Above *A nineteenth-century view of the port of Le Havre.*

There is also a vast out-of-town shopping centre, which is very convenient, but leaves the centre apart from the port activity a little dead. Like many ports Le Havre has a slight air of gloom, but its importance to French life and economy cannot be doubted.

The mudflats and sandbanks stretch out towards the sea just a little way beyond Le Havre. As the great ocean-going ships thread endlessly in and out of the swirling waters of the English Channel, no one can say exactly where the Seine ends, or where the waters which have given France so much find their final resting place in the endless sea.

– Le Havre was a planned port. It was built in the late sixteenth century on marshland to replace the declining port of Honfleur. Many famous voyages of discovery, such as Champlain's voyage to Canada in 1602, were made from here. Today the port has an immense harbour with hundreds of ships standing on the quays and vast sheds which are large enough to house tropical trees shipped from South America ·or Africa. In September 1944 the city suffered much damage, as did many other cities along the Seine, because the German invaders were determined to fight to the bitter end. Since then the town has been completely rebuilt, although the stone buildings can seem a little monotonous to those who do not like modern architecture.

Below *An aerial view of the modern seaport of Le Havre, which was almost completely rebuilt after the Second World War.*

Journey's end — a far cry from the Seine's humble beginnings in the heart of France.

Glossary

Bargee   A person who lives on a barge.

Bore   A tidal flood which rushes with great violence up the estuaries of some rivers at certain times of the year.

Château   One of the castles, country houses or mansions for which France is well known.

Cutting   A channel which is cut beside a river to bypass a difficult section of the river and make navigation easier.

Embankment   An artificial or natural barrier along a river bank, which protects low-lying land along the river from flooding.

Estuary   The widening channel of a river where it nears the sea.

Impressionists   A group of nineteenth-century painters, including Monet, Manet, Renoir, and Sisley, who were interested in conveying experience by painting fleeting impressions of an object. These painters were particularly fascinated by the effect of light on water.

Meander   A bend in a river.

New town   A town that has been planned and built by the government to accommodate overspill from a nearby town or city.

Plateau   An area of high, flat land.

Pointillism   A style of painting in which dots of unmixed colour are painted on a white background so that when viewed from a distance the separate colours seem to merge into each other.

Province   France is divided into regions, called provinces, such as the Île de France, Burgundy and Normandy.

Sandbank   An underwater bank of sand in the sea, which may become exposed at low tide.

Silt   A fine deposit of mud or clay carried down by a river, which may cause the delta of the river or stream to become filled up or silted.

Towpath   A path beside a canal or river, used by people or animals towing boats or barges.

Tributary   A stream or river that flows into another larger one.

Facts and figures

Length: 780 km (485 miles)
Drainage basin: 78,000 square km (30,000 square miles)
Average flow at Paris: 1000 cubic metres (10,000 cubic feet) per second
Freight carried: 40,000,000 tonnes (in 1975)

Some important dates

c. 50 B.C. to A.D. 400   Age of the Roman Empire in France. Many cities and monuments were founded along the Seine during this time.

c. 1000 to A.D. 1500   Medieval period. French kings established Paris as the capital of France and civilization flourished in the valley of the Seine.

1789–1799   Period of the French Revolution. The French monarchy was deposed and a Republic was set up in its place.

1939–1945   Second World War. France was occupied by German invaders from 1940 to 1944, and many of the cities along the Seine were destroyed or damaged.

Further reading

Chelminski, Rudolf *The Great Cities: Paris* (Time Life, 1977).

Gibbings, R. *Coming Down the Seine* (Dent and Sons, 1953).

Glyn, Anthony *The Seine* (Weidenfeld and Nicolson, 1966).

Lifhitz, Danielle *France; The Land and its People* (Macdonald Countries, Silver Burdett, 1973).

Wilson, Hazel *The Seine: River of Paris* (Frederick Muller, 1962; Gerrard Publishing Co, 1962).

ACKNOWLEDGEMENTS

J. Allan Cash *frontispiece*, 9, 11, 13, 14, 16, 23, 60; Collection of the Art Institute of Chicago 35; Colour Library International 25 (bottom), 30, 31 (top); James Davis 29; Documentation Française, Paris 21, 22, 25 (top), 26, 32, 50 (bottom), 58, 62, 63; Mary Evans Picture Library 28; C. Gibb 8, 31 (bottom), 44, 47; National Gallery, London 10, 18, 43; Alan Hutchinson 12, 15; Mansell Collection 17, 24, 36, 49, 50 (top), 62; John Topham Picture Library 19, 20, 27, 33, 39, 46, 55, 56; T. A. Wilkie 37, 38 (both), 40, 41, 42, 43, 45, 48, 51, 53, 54, 57, 59, 61.

Special thanks to Alan Gunston for the mapwork.

Index

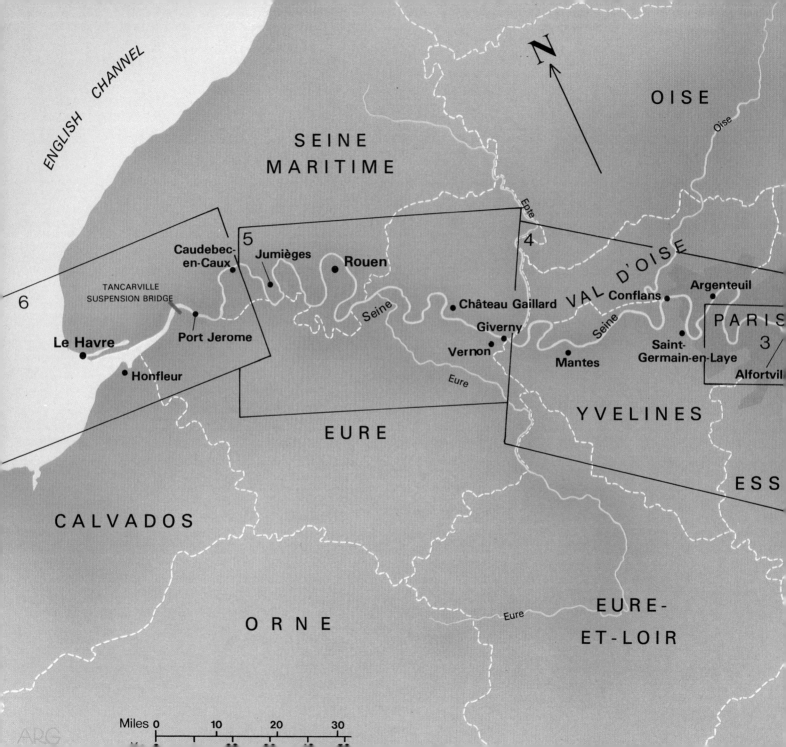

ENGLISH CHANNEL

N

OISE

Oise

SEINE
MARITIME

6

5

Caudebec-
en-Caux

Jumièges

Rouen

TANCARVILLE
SUSPENSION BRIDGE

Port Jerome

Le Havre

Honfleur

Seine

4

VAL D'OISE

Château Gaillard

Giverny

Vernon

Eure

Conflans

Argenteuil

Seine

Saint-
Germain-en-Laye

Mantes

PARIS

3

Alfortville

CALVADOS

YVELINES

EURE

ESS

ORNE

Eure

EURE-
ET-LOIR

ARG

Miles 0   10   20   30

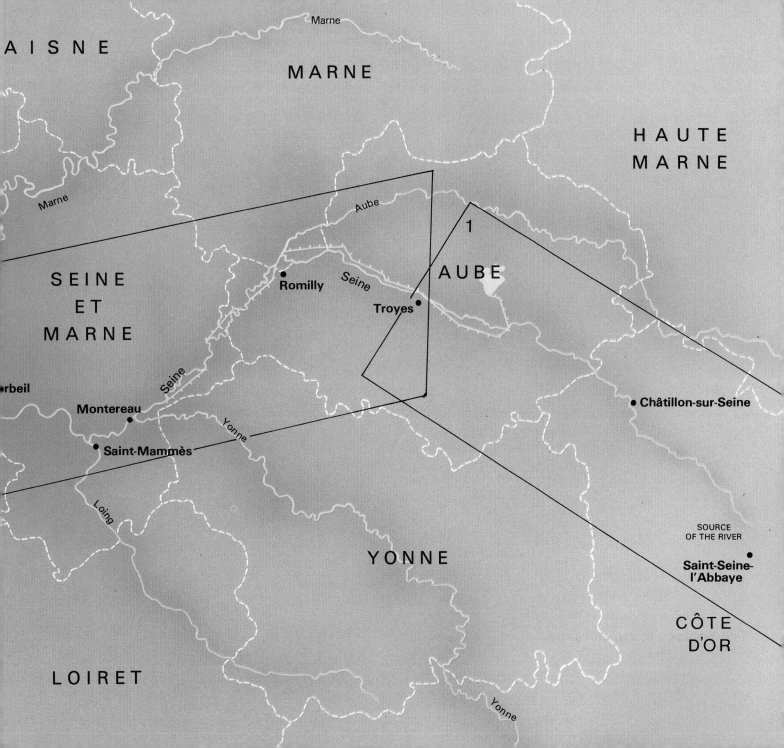